# The Complete Guide to Money Laundering

Table of Contents

The Complete Guide to Money Laundering

There are many benefits to living in America which is often referred to as the land of opportunity. Many people take great lengths to get here. We are the home of the entrepreneur. Millionaires are made every day in various ways and methods. What most of these millionaires and billionaires have in common is they know how to hide assets and avoid paying taxes just ask our new President Donald J. Trump he is a master at this shell game and is rich beyond any of our wildest dreams.

First of all this is my disclaimer:

I will reveal the methods used by the rich and powerful and elite. I am not encouraging anyone to use them. I will not be a co-defendant or accomplice to any activities that arise from me providing knowledge or information. I am just the messenger providing techniques used by powerful businessmen, drug dealers, cartels, and corporations.

My goal is to unravel the mysteries and methods used to achieve vast amounts of wealth by the all mighty and all-powerful 1% that control 100% of the world's wealth.

This is a general guide or how to launder money also known as make it disappear. I will not go into detail step by step instructions some imagination is required and if you choose to apply these methods they are at your own risk so if you find yourself behind bars don't write me or as me for legal advice I am not a lawyer I am only a writer providing historically relevant facts

I am prepared to reveal the secrets of the rich and famous which under penalty of law are considered illegal in the United States of America.

So listen up and take notice as I open your eyes to the world of money laundering..........

# Safes

There are various types of safes. There are the traditional safes which require a hiding place within your home. There are hidden object safes available online many in the forms of books, clocks and various other everyday objects found in homes.

Property can also be used a safe. Homes, Apartments, Storage Units, and Vehicles.

Cars are very good places to hide money if they are located in a safe place. They are often not included in search warrants so a vehicle parked on a property or inside a property is often off limits unless specified in a search warrant unless you are driving it or are inside of it while a search warrant is being executed because evidence within it allow for a probable cause search because evidence can be hidden during an arrest or investigation.

Homes, Apartments, and Storage units are also a good place to store large sums of cash. These require limited access and knowledge of their existence.

One safe that I haven't mentioned is a safety deposit box.

Banks charge monthly or yearly fees but your money jewelry and valuables can be safely tucked away inside a banking institution of your choosing.

Which leads me to the next way to safely launder your money. Putting small amounts of money in various different banks is another method used to avoid suspicion. Small deposits periodically won't set off any alarms if your balance stays below $10,000.

Another way that people have commonly adapted to laundering money is a front which is basically a small business that takes in cash which in not often recorded or taxed. Family owned small businesses are often the best fronts such as barbershops, restaurants, bars, clubs and car washes.

# Used Cars

Buying and selling used cars is also an excellent front. Cars hold value and can be easily converted to cash by selling it. Cars are valuable assets because they are mobile safes. Motor vehicles can be put in a wife or other family members name for ownership and cannot be easily connected to another person even though they can drive or retain it at any time making them a prized possession. They can also be insured if needed to avoid any financial loss.

# Property

Homes are a great investment and can be rented or sold for more than originally purchased. They can be used as shelter or stashing large amounts of money. The term "stash house" is often used as a description of a housing unit used to stockpile cash. Drug dealers and cartels often use "stash houses" for storage, transportation, and the counting of currency. There is risk involved with stashing money in property but often the reward is worth the risk as long as laundering activities are not detected by armed robbers or law enforcement. Homes can also be insured to avoid financial loss due to unforeseen events such as break ins fires or floods.

# Jewelry

Jewelry is often a good investment that retains or increases in value. It must be held in a very safe location in your home. A safe or safety deposit box is a must. Jewelry can also be converted to cash and can also be relocated if there is a clear and present danger to outside elements. Jewelry can also be insured in case of robbery or theft avoiding risk and financial loss.

# Family & Friends

Trusted family and friends can also hold assets including money for you. This is often risky due to human nature but having someone you can trust is one of the most treasured resources to have. Most of the time they want to be compensated for their efforts but it helps to insure and create a bond of trust. I  would definitely weigh this option and only allow them to have a limited amount of money in their control and have the money in a safe where they have limited access to or in case of an emergency situation. Never give them more money than you can afford to lose just in case they become untrustworthy.

# Prepaid Credit Cards

Prepaid Credit Cards are easily accessible and can be found in just about every grocery, dollar and department store I have even seen them in Dollar Tree. They can be a very valued tool. They are a very small and easily accessible and just about anytime day or night. Most can hold up to $5000. Due to their size they can be easily hidden which is an excellent method of money laundering. Seriously think about it 20 cards holding $5000 is equal to $100,000. Cartels have used them to bring $8 to $24 billon across the United States border annually. Many ATMs can be used to withdraw cash using prepaid credit cards and most businesses take credit card payments.

# Money Orders

Money orders can easily be transferred to cash and can also hold sums of money up to $5000.They can be held in wallets and various other modes of transportation including via US or international mail. They can easily be converted to cash and even cashed in ATM and withdrawn in cash increments. They are relatively easy to cash in banks and other institutions that accept them in major retail chains such that accept Money Gram Western Union and United States Postal Money Orders based on your geographical location other money order carriers may apply based on cash availability and the amount of the money order. Also there are many check cashing places that offer free money orders.

# The Internet

Now that we are in the digital age money laundering is also adapting. Money can be transferred into PayPal and various other similar payment methods including :

Amazon Payments

Apple Pay

Bitcoin

Google Wallet

WorldPay

Paypay by Ebay is the most popular to date and and I have recently become aware that they even have an option that allow for transferred money to accrue interest. It is not FDIC insured but PayPal is a relatively secure company and the top online payment service from a risk management aspect.

There are various other methods to launder money through legal and illegal means. Again I do not encourage anyone to engage in any illegal activities. This is written to educate and make aware of methods that have been used historically by the elite and the illegal to cut corners and accumulate large amounts of money to avoid taxation and detection. So unless you are a drug dealer, mobster, politician, millionaire or billionaire businessman with a top notch attorney I suggest you don't attempt to defraud or engage in a pattern of corrupt activities of money laundering under penalty of law. Think of this in the same manners as the Surgeon General Warning smokers of the potential risks of their behaviors. So if you decide to disregard my warning don't come knocking at my door or trying to make me part of your decision making process. This is a free country and I am merely expressing my Freedom of Speech afforded to me by the United States Constitution.

God Bless America

Don't Be Try to be the Next El Chapo or Scarface

Author TJ Clemons

I will not be sending any bond money or legal advice. I am not a bondsman or an attorney. I hope you enjoyed this book and are more educated in the art of money laundering. It will forever be a part of our culture and history in this great country. Just don't fall victim to it's seductive lure. It is for the powerful and select who have access to the best legal protection under our system of justice. They have and they will continue to break the rules for monetary gain and accumulate vast sums of currency and control with their power and influence. Thank you for purchasing this cherished information and hope it doesn't fall into the hands of a criminal mastermind. This is an informative and enlightening look into the world of money laundering for entertainment purposes only. I sincerely hope that you have a better understanding of the money laundering process. It has been my goal to enlighten and entertain avid enthusiasts of the money laundering domain.

Made in the USA
Las Vegas, NV
01 December 2023